YOUR KNOWLEDGE HAS VALUE

Walter Washington

Public Administration Defined within the Context of its Four Frames and Pros and Cons to Privatization

GRIN Verlag

Bibliografische Information der Deutschen Nationalbibliothek:

Die Deutsche Bibliothek verzeichnet diese Publikation in der Deutschen National-
bibliografie; detaillierte bibliografische Daten sind im Internet über http://dnb.d-
nb.de/ abrufbar.

Imprint:

Copyright © 2014 GRIN Verlag GmbH
Druck und Bindung: Books on Demand GmbH, Norderstedt Germany
ISBN: 978-3-656-61097-7

This book at GRIN:

http://www.grin.com/en/e-book/269828/public-administration-defined-within-the-
context-of-its-four-frames-and

Public Administration Defined within the Context of its Four Frames

– And –

Pros and Cons to Privatization

By Walter L. Washington, Jr.

Public Administration Defined within the Context of its Four Frames

How is public administration defined within the context of its four frames? Before answering this question, first think about how public administration is defined in general. Public administration is a system of public servants managing an array of services, programs, and other related actions that occur in the public sector, whether that is government, nonprofit, and in other cases, nongovernmental or not-for-profit organizations. This level of management is extremely necessary in order for much of everyday society to operate, however, it is also even more necessary that those administrating those services ensure that they are component, fair, and just individuals or groups who hold at least a reasonable amount of knowledge and expertise in order to effectively administer said services to its respective recipients. This exchange of services from the servicer or service provider to client/customer/service recipient, in theory, can have a reciprocal effect in way that allows the utmost effectiveness in the process overall. Everyday life provides a great amount of situations that involved public administration, which leads into the four frames of public administration, and of the four, three are mentioned in course text.

David Rosenbloom of American University has argued that these three functions of government [individualism, equality, and liberty] are related to three views of the role of public administrators in American society (Rosenbloom, 1993, p. 15):

    1.   The managerial approach to public administration, which Rosenbloom connects to the executive function, emphasizes the management and organization of public organizations. As with Wilson, this view sometimes

suggests that management in the public sector is very much like that in the private sector; that is, it is primarily concerned with efficiency.

2.   The political approach to public administration, related to the legislative function in government, is more concerned about ensuring constitutional safeguards, such as those already mentioned. Efficiency becomes less a concern than effectiveness or responsiveness.

3.   Finally, the legal approach to public administration, related to the judicial function, emphasizes the administrator's role in applying and enforcing the law in specific situations. It is also concerned with the adjudicatory role of public organizations.

(Denhardt, Denhardt, & Blanc, 2013, p. 3-4)

The fourth frame of public administration is "occupational" and per the notes from class, this frame is labeled by some as "market". The occupational approach to public administration, related to various functions such as work-related, professional, and industrial, emphasizes the range of fields of public administration, which the in-classroom instruction (Waters, 2014) present these fields as the following:

* Social welfare   * Engineering   * Others

* Economics   * Security

* Health   * Safety

When referring to these frames of public administration in comparison to real, live scenarios, one example that could be used could be that of a governing body of a small-to-medium sized locality. This locality's name (for sake of demonstrative purposes) is "Publictopia", which has a city manager, a board of directors, city court system, and various departments and divisions such as fire, police, and parks. The city manager typically is set in the managerial frame of mind because of the "executive function" that "emphasizes management and organization" of "the written [policies], procedures, laws" and etcetera; whereas, the board of directors usually are structured with a political frame of mind that accentuates "effectiveness over efficiency" with an outlook "about doing collectively what cannot be done individually." The city court system's role in all of this "deals with applying and enforcing the specific law", while "mainly [dealing] with [the] enforcement of policies developed through city manager (managerial) and the board of directors (political). Lastly, various departments and divisions display the occupational frame of mind with a number of "fields of public administration". In theory, "Publictopia" should be an effective, efficient, and organized locality that expresses a reciprocal relationship between the ones who govern and the ones who are governed, however, in true and practical application, this level of effectiveness, efficiency, and organization may not be as great as it is designed to be. People will be people and this is a testament of what actually happens (rather than what should happen) within the four frames of public administration.

Pros and Cons to Privatization

Privatization at first glance may possibly give some people the appearance that it has little or nothing to do with the public sector and public administration, thus quite possibly making it appear to deal more or exclusively with the private sector. This appearance is not quite all true and it is not quite all false because it can coexist in between both facets of the public and private sectors, therefore making it a prospective example of one frame of public administration, political, which is "about doing collectively what cannot be done individually". (Waters, 2014) This concept is widely utilized in a range of areas of public administration. According to Denhardt, Denhardt, and Blanc, privatization is "the use of NGOs [nongovernmental organizations] to provide goods or services previously provided by government." (Denhardt, Denhardt, & Blanc, 2013, p. 109) These nongovernmental organizations or NGOs for short can include religious organizations, nonprofits, and private business, although in some perspectives, NGOs could easily include some political action committees, lobbying organizations, and special interest groups, it all just depends on each individual group's scope. Through the utilization of privatization, the public sector can broaden its scope of services especially in the instance when those services require specific levels of expertise that would be difficult to muster had it be solely on the shoulders of the public sector if they had to face it alone. "In its broader sense, privatization refers to efforts to remove government from any involvement in either the design or conduct of a particular service." (Denhardt, Denhardt, & Blanc, 2013, p. 109) In this sense, while the effort may be to remove government, it should be acknowledged that although government might be removed from providing direct services it is not completely removed altogether. In many cases, it is the government who still provides access to the funding needed for the NGOs to complete what needs to be accomplished in order to meet the needs and demands of those requiring those now outsourced services. When analyzing privatization, like when making any other rational analysis it is strongly recommended to compare and contrast the pros and cons.

Pros

* "People may feel that clients will receive more personal attention from a nongovernmental or private group" (Denhardt, Denhardt, & Blanc, 2013, p. 110)
* Private firms may operate more efficiently when public programs may seem inappropriate to government or other related instances
* Removes government from providing direct services and replaces them with industry experts who have more expertise in the respective field of services being provided
* Provides recipients with improved services
* "Enhances competition among service providers, thus ensuring that the new means of delivering services will provide higher quality at a lower cost to the client" (Denhardt, Denhardt, & Blanc, 2013, p. 110)

These pros of privatization provide only a limited insight to the benefits of privatization and how it can work for all parties involved, however, not all ideas and practices are free of flaws, and therefore the cons of privatization are listed below to highlight a limited insight into privatization and how it could detrimental to all parties involved.

Cons

* "Privatization of human services has its challenges…a closer look reveals major problems relating to sustainability" (Denhardt, Denhardt, & Blanc, 2013, p. 111)
* The intentions of the private firm may not parallel with the government's objectives and its taxpayers' exact needs
* Could potentially be more harmful than good due to possible negative attributes such as lack of ethical decision making, deregulations, and poor accountability
* May have been forcibly used without the support of the stakeholders
* If due diligence is forgo, ill-equipped contractors are chosen, and progress is failed to be monitored, then outsourcing deals can turn into costly disasters (Denhardt, Denhardt, & Blanc, 2013, p. 112)

Through the explanation of just some of the pros and cons of privatization that were abovementioned, each also includes some of the ways privatization is handled. Further illustration of some of the ways privatization is handled can be seen throughout the various levels of government. The military's use of contracts for equipment and manufacturing is one example on the federal level. A state's contract with contractors to construct a respective state's portion of interstates is an example on the state level. A county or city's use of an advertising company to promote and/or enhance their respective locality's image is an example of the local level. Upon reviewing these examples, it is just as important to review and recognize the major types of players such as the various levels of government, the people those various levels of government serve, and the nongovernmental organizations involved. Moreover, it is also important to include what important steps government must include in the process just as the Privatization Task Force created by New Jersey governor Chris Christie notes, which is "that care must be taken in the process of privatization... While the government has increasingly served as a broker of services, that new role bears special responsibilities." (Denhardt, Denhardt, & Blanc, 2013, p. 112) This taskforce also reported that the states most successful in privatization created a permanent, centralized entity to manage and oversee the operation, from project analysis and vendor selection to contracting and procurement" ("The Pros and Cons of Privatizing," 2010). (Denhardt, Denhardt, & Blanc, 2013, p. 112) At any level of government, it must acknowledge that there is a variety of mechanisms available to be utilized in the privatization process. Through defining the problem, planning, developing strategies, contracting, forming partnerships, and signing memorandums of understanding, the privatization process is implemented, executed, and commenced, although, these are just a number of steps government must include in the process.

References

Denhardt, R. B., Denhardt, J. V., & Blanc, T. A. (2013). Personal Action in Public Organizations. In *Public administration: An action orientation* (pp. 3 - 4).

Denhardt, R. B., Denhardt, J. V., & Blanc, T. A. (2013). The Interorganizational Context of Public Administration. In *Public administration: An action orientation* (pp. 109 - 112).

Waters, M. A. (2014). Chapter 1 & 2 [PowerPoint slides]. Retrieved from in-classroom printed handout

Waters, M. A. (2014). Chapter 3 & 4 [PowerPoint slides]. Retrieved from in-classroom printed handout